Friendship Fun!

Contributing Designers

Phyllis Dunstan

Trena Hegdahl

Mary Beth Janssen-Fleischman

Kim Solga

Publications International, Ltd.

Craft Designers:

Phyllis Dunstan is a partner in a personalized design firm specializing in theme decorating and gift wrapping. She is a member of the Peninsula Stitchery Guild and other craft organizations. Her creations have been seen extensively in national publications and have appeared on numerous magazine covers. Her designs appear on pages 8, 10, 16, and 25.

Trena Hegdahl is owner and primary designer for the firm of Mine & Yours, creating wearables and other projects. Her work has been shown extensively on television and in numerous publications, including *Treasury of Country Cooking & Crafts* and *Creative Activity Kit: Bible Crafts*. Her design appears on page 42.

Mary Beth Janssen-Fleischman is a hair and beauty industry professional with film and television credits. She has contributed to a variety of magazines, including *Modern Salon, Harper's Bazaar,* and *Coiffure de Paris.* She has served as a contributing writer and hair designer for numerous hairstyle books, including *Beautiful Braids.* Her hair design appears on page 32.

Kim Solga is a writer and crafter who specializes in children's arts and crafts. She publishes books for teaching art, sells child-safe art supplies throughout the world, and has authored or contributed to several arts and activity books for children, including *Creative Activity Kit: Nature Crafts.* Her designs appear on pages 13, 29, 36, 39, 44, and 46.

Photography: Brian Warling
Stylist: Danita Wiecek
Technical Advisor: Christine DeJulio
Models: Royal Model Management, Inc.: Bonney Bowman, Stefanie Leafblad, Brittany Marques, Tierra Smith, Rylee Stull, Anna Wilson

Special thanks for their pictures to Aja Aktay, Kimberly Andrews, Alyssa Conner, Chloe Gassney, Laine Marsh, Rachel Marsh, Ashley Psichalinos, Aimee Rambo, Alyssa Rambo.

Source of Materials
The following products were used for the projects in this book: Tulip Productions: Bead Colorpoint paints: 10; Slick paints: 16, 25.

Louis Weber, C.E.O.
Publications International, Ltd.
7373 North Cicero Avenue
Lincolnwood, Illinois 60712

Permission is never granted for commercial purposes.

Manufactured in China.

8 7 6 5 4 3 2 1

ISBN: 0-7853-2324-4

contents

Introduction

Dear Parents and Teachers—

We know that most kids will be able to make the projects with little help, but there will be times when your assistance is needed. If the child has never used a glue gun, explain that the nozzle and freshly applied glue are warm, even when set on low. Have a glass of water nearby just in case warm fingers need cooling.

You know your child's abilities—craft knives are very sharp and you should judge whether your child is able to handle one safely. Some project instructions direct the child to ask for adult help. Also, be sure everyone understands the "Important Things to Know!" section in this introduction.

Most important, this should be an enjoyable, creative experience. Although we provide specific instructions, it's wonderful to see children create their own versions. ENJOY!

Hey, Kids—

With *Friendship Fun!*, you can make any rainy day fun! This book will show you how to make great presents for your friends, friendship bracelets, cool T-shirts, and much, much more.

Friendship Fun! was made with you in mind. Many of the projects are fun things you can make by yourself. However, for some projects, you will need to ask an adult for help.

It's a good idea to make a project for the first time following the instructions exactly. Then, feel free to make another, using your imagination, changing colors, adding a bit of yourself to make it even more yours. Think of all the variations you can make and all the gifts you can give!

Most important, HAVE FUN! Think how proud you'll be to say, "I made this myself!"

Important Things to Know!

Although we know you'll want to get started right away, please read these few basic steps before beginning:

1. Go through the book and decide what project you want to make first. Read the materials list and the instructions completely.

2. Gather all your materials, remembering to ask permission! If you need to purchase materials, take along your book or make a shopping list so you know exactly what you need.

3. Prepare your work area ahead of time. Cleanup will be easier if you prepare first!

4. Be sure that an adult is nearby to offer help if you need it. Adult assistance is needed if you will be using a glue gun, a craft knife, the oven, or anything else that may be dangerous!

5. Be careful not to put any materials near your mouth. Watch out for small items, like beads, around little kids and pets.

6. Use a low-temperature glue gun. Do not touch the nozzle or freshly applied glue, because it may still be hot. Use the glue gun with adult permission only!

7. Wear an apron when painting with acrylic paints, because after the paint dries, it is permanent. If you do get it on your clothes, wash with soap and warm water immediately.

8. When the instructions direct you to paint two coats of a color, let the first coat dry before painting the second.

9. Clean up afterward, and put away all materials and tools.

So grab your best friend, ask an adult for the supplies and a little bit of help, get your work area ready, and happy crafting!

painted plates with pizzazz!

Make these
fun plates
at your next
slumber
party. Your
party will
be the talk
of the
neighborhood!

*Friendship is the only element that
will ever hold the world together.*
—Woodrow Wilson

5

What You'll Need

Glass plates

Heat-tempering paint: orange, bright blue, bright purple, aqua (We used Liquitex Glossies Acrylic Enamels, available in art supply stores.)

Paintbrushes: #1 liner, ¼-inch flat

Tools: *paper towels, vinegar, tracing paper, pencil, clear tape, disposable plate*

1. Wash the glass plates in soap and water. Make a mixture of 50 percent water and 50 percent vinegar, and wash it over the surface. Do not touch where you will be painting—the oil from your skin will keep the paint from sticking to the glass.

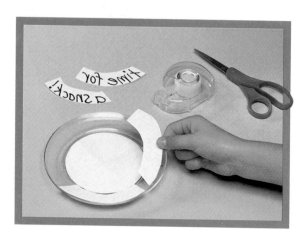

2. Either photocopy or trace the pattern from the book. You may need to enlarge or reduce it to fit the size of your plates. Tape the pattern to the front of the plate. You will be painting on the back of the plate.

3. Use a disposable plate for a palette. Squirt a bit of each color on your plate. Begin painting in the center of the plate. Try to keep a medium coat of paint—too much will bubble when you bake it and thin coats will wash off too easily. Use the flat brush for thicker lines and the liner brush for thinner lines. Be sure to let each color dry before you paint the next. Also, if you touch the plate, rerinse with the vinegar and water.

4. A tip for painting the outer ring of the plate is to set it on top of a bowl. Then you can turn the bowl and not smear the paint.

5. Get an adult to help you with this step! Preheat your oven to 325°F. Place your plates painted side up on a cookie sheet. Bake the plates for 30 to 40 minutes—be sure your kitchen is well ventilated! Do not bake at a higher temperature or for too short a time. Your dishes are now dishwasher safe!

extra idea!

Paint a "Happy Birthday" or "Get Well" plate for your best friend. Pile it up with her favorite cookies for a great surprise treat!

frame-ingly
beautiful!

The only reward of virtue is virtue; the only way to have a friend is to be one.
—Ralph Waldo Emerson

(glue tab)

Put a picture of your best friend in this frame to remember a special time with her. Colorful buttons add flair!

photostand pattern

(glue tab)

What You'll Need

Buttons in various sizes and colors

8×10-inch white photo mat with oval opening

Embroidery floss to match button colors

8×10-inch cardboard backing, medium weight

9×4-inch cardboard, medium weight

2 yellow plastic report holders

Tools: *craft glue, craft stick, pencil, tracing paper, heavy scissors or utility knife*

1. Arrange the buttons around the oval opening of the photo mat. Be sure to mix the colors and sizes of the buttons. Thread embroidery floss through the holes of the larger buttons and tie the ends together on top. Trim the ends of the floss.

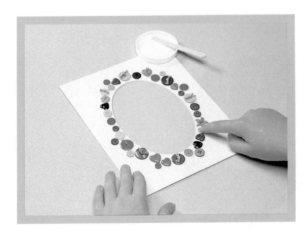

2. Apply glue to the backs of the buttons with the craft stick. Replace buttons on the mat.

3. Trace the photostand pattern onto the small cardboard and cut out. Using the tip of a pair of scissors, score the stand on the dotted lines. Fold the scored portion back. Center the stand on the back of the cardboard backing. Glue the bottom glue tab to the bottom edge of cardboard and the top glue tab to the center back.

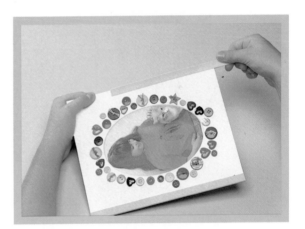

4. When the glue is dry, place your photo between the oval mat and the backing cardboard. With the help of an adult, cut the plastic report holders to 10 inches. Slide a yellow report holder over each side of the frame.

cookie cutter
cards

True happiness
Consists not in the multitude of friends,
But in the worth and choice.
—Ben Jonson

Use Mom's cookie cutters to create quick and easy notecards for a friend. Dots of silver add extra sparkle!

What You'll Need

Brightly colored cardstock
Brightly colored paper
Assorted cookie cutters
Silver glitter paint
Tools: *pencil, tracing paper, scissors, cardboard, craft glue, craft stick*

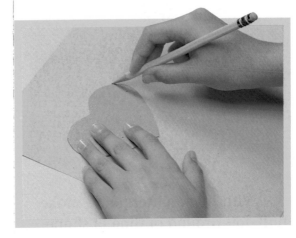

1. Cut cardstock to desired size. Fold the sheet in half.

3. If you don't have cookie cutters, you can trace or photocopy the patterns from this book and make templates out of cardboard. Trace around the templates onto the colored paper and cut out.

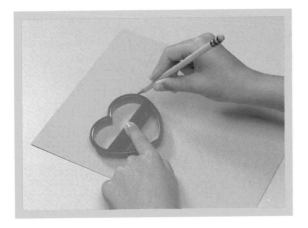

4. Using the craft stick, spread glue on the back of cutout shape. Glue shape to the front of the card. Let glue dry.

2. Place cookie cutter on top of colored paper and trace around it. Cut out shape.

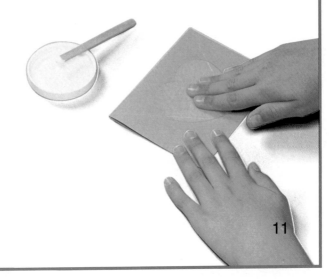

5. With silver glitter paint, make small dots around outline of shape. Let paint dry completely.

lovable
teddy bear
plaque

This fuzzy teddy framed with lace carries a special message for your favorite friend.

What You'll Need

4½-inch square of foam board (or wood)

Fine-tip markers: dark blue, medium blue, green, red, yellow

4 light blue poms: 1 inch, ¾ inch, two ½ inch

4 dark blue poms, ½ inch each

2 blue wiggly eyes

1 tiny red pom

½ yard ruffled lace trim

6 inches ribbon

Tools: tracing paper, transfer paper, tape, pencil, cool-temp glue gun, glue sticks

1. Trace or photocopy the pattern on page 15. Place the pattern on the foam board or wood plaque over the transfer paper and tape the papers down so they won't wiggle.

2. Trace over the pattern with a pencil to transfer the lines onto your plaque. Remove tape and papers.

What do we live for, if it is not to make life less difficult for each other?
—George Eliot

3. Use the medium blue marker to draw the letters of the message. Add dots at the corners of the letters with the dark blue marker.

4. Draw the flower stems with the green marker. Add red and yellow dot flowers.

5. Glue the poms onto the plaque to create the teddy bear. Start with the body (1-inch pom) and head (¾-inch pom). Add the arms and legs (dark blue ½-inch poms) and ears (light blue ½-inch poms). Finally, glue 2 wiggly eyes and the tiny red pom nose onto the head pom.

6. Ask for adult help here. To add ruffled lace, apply glue to 3-inch lengths along the back edge of the plaque. Press lace into glue. Be very careful, even a cool-temp glue gun gets very hot! Continue gluing 3-inch sections until the lace is attached all around the plaque. Overlap the ends ½ inch and tack the lace ends together with a dot of glue.

7. Glue a loop of ribbon on the top back of the plaque to make a hanger. If you've used a wooden plaque, hammer a thumbtack through the ribbons to help secure them.

photo tag
necklace

Take your friends with you wherever you go! Make the arrow pin out of cardboard and key tags for a cool option!

What You'll Need

Small piece of cardboard
Photos of friends
Key tags (available at hardware stores)
1 yard yellow cotton cording
¼ yard each of red, orange, and green satin ribbon, ¹⁄₁₆ inch wide

Tools: *tracing paper, pencil, scissors, tacky glue, paper punch, ruler*

Yes'm, old friends is always best, 'less you can catch a new one that's fit to make an old one out of.

—Sarah Orne Jewett

1. Trace circle pattern onto cardboard and cut out. Center circle over your photo and trace with a sharp pencil. Cut out photo circle. (Tip: To cut a smooth circle, hold the scissors still while you turn the photo. Practice on scrap paper.) Cut out as many photos as you need.

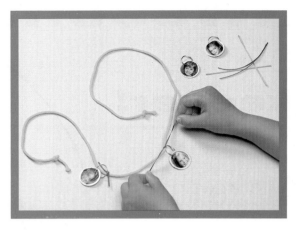

3. Tie a knot at each end of yellow cording. Cut the satin ribbon into 4-inch lengths. Slip a piece of ribbon through the ring on the tag and tie the ring to the center of the yellow cord with a double knot. Trim ends of ribbon. Repeat for all photo tags, using all the ribbon colors.

2. Remove the ring from a key tag and apply glue to one side of the tag. Lay the photo over the tag, making sure the hole in the tag is at the top. Repeat with all photos. Let glue dry. Using the hole in the tag as a guide, punch a hole through the photo with the paper punch. Replace the ring. Prepare all photo tags.

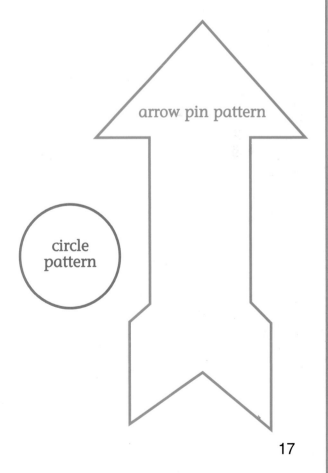

arrow pin pattern

circle pattern

awesome
earring
keeper!

Make this fantastic earring keeper for a friend's birthday!

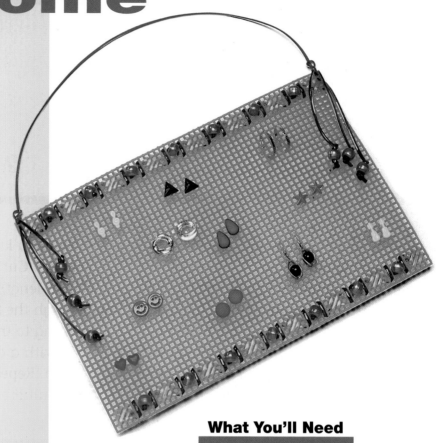

extra idea!
Be creative! Make an earring holder using your own designs!

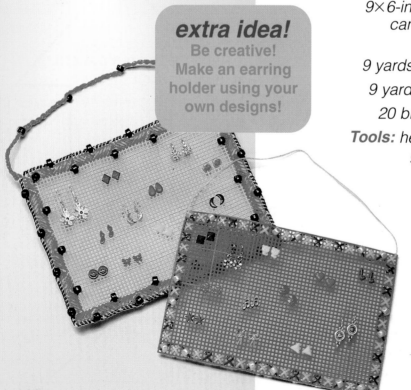

What You'll Need

9×6-inch piece of hot pink plastic canvas, 60 holes wide and 40 holes high

9 yards clear yellow lanyard lacing

9 yards clear blue lanyard lacing

20 blue pearlized pony beads

Tools: heavy-duty scissors, cool-temp glue gun, glue sticks

A true friend is the best Possession.
—Benjamin Franklin

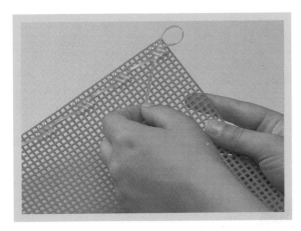

1. When working with lanyard lacing, check after every stitch to make sure the lacing isn't twisted. When you start stitching, leave a small tail and stitch over it to hold the lacing in place. At the end of your row, or when you run out of lacing, push the remaining lacing under stitches on back. Trim the tail. If the lacing doesn't stay put, put a small dab of glue on the end. Be careful, even cool-temp glue gets very hot! Ask an adult for help.

2. Adding beads is very simple. Just slip a bead on when you have the lacing on the front side of your piece.

3. Make the handle about 10 inches longer than you want it to be. Slide an end of the lacing through the top right hole of your piece. Tie a knot, leaving a 5-inch tail on the front. Tie a knot above where you want to place a bead, slip on the bead and then tie a knot below the bead. Repeat for the other side.

4. Cut two 9-inch pieces of lacing. From the back, slip an end of the lacing through the top right hole and the other end through the hole directly beneath it. Repeat the same procedure as above for adding beads. Repeat for the left side of the holder.

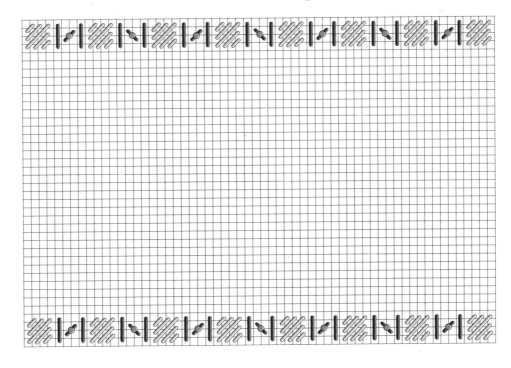

These cookies would be great fun to make with your best friend. You make the chocolate cookie dough, and she'll make the peanut butter. Then swap heart centers!

heart of my heart cookies

1 recipe Chocolate Cookie
    Dough
½ cup creamy peanut butter
½ cup shortening
1 cup granulated sugar
1 egg
1 teaspoon vanilla
3 tablespoons milk
2 cups flour
1 teaspoon baking powder
¼ teaspoon salt

1. Prepare Chocolate Cookie Dough as directed. Divide dough into 2 portions; chill 2 hours.

2. Cream peanut butter, shortening, and sugar in electric mixer until light and fluffy. Add egg and vanilla; mix until well blended. Add milk; mix well. Add flour, baking powder, and salt. Mix at low speed until well blended. Divide into 2 portions; chill 1 to 2 hours.

3. Heat oven to 350°F. Roll 1 portion of peanut butter dough on floured waxed paper to 3/16-inch thickness. Cut with heart-shaped cookie cutters. Transfer to lightly greased cookie sheet. Use a smaller heart-shaped cookie cutter to remove a small section from center of heart; set smaller cutout aside.

4. Repeat with chocolate dough. If dough becomes too soft, place in freezer for 5 minutes before transferring to cookie sheet. Place small cutouts into opposite dough; press lightly.

5. Bake 12 to 14 minutes or just until edges are lightly browned. Cool; transfer to a wire rack. Cool completely.

Makes 4 dozen 3-inch cookies

When friends meet, hearts warm.
—Proverb

Chocolate Cookie Dough

1 cup butter or margarine,
    softened
1 cup sugar
1 egg
1 teaspoon vanilla
2 ounces semisweet
    chocolate, melted
2¼ cups all-purpose flour
1 teaspoon baking powder
¼ teaspoon salt

Beat butter and sugar in large bowl at high speed of electric mixer until fluffy. Beat in egg and vanilla. Add melted chocolate; mix well. Add flour, baking powder, and salt. Mix at low speed until well blended.

best buds

Glue the picture of your best friend to one flower and yourself to another, and you'll have a keepsake you'll treasure forever!

Flowers are lovely;
love is flower-like;
Friendship is a sheltering tree.
—Samuel Coleridge

Best Buds!

What You'll Need

8 craft sticks

Felt: green, teal, purple, hot pink, and fuchsia

2 chenille stems

***Tools:** craft glue, scissors, pencil, tracing paper, pins, black marker*

1. Take 6 of the craft sticks and arrange them to resemble a picket fence (3 up and down, and 3 across). Glue the sticks into place, using a craft stick to apply the glue. Cut a piece of green felt to fit behind the piece you have made. Glue felt to the back of the fence.

2. Trace the patterns from this book. Cut out the patterns and pin them to the felt colors pictured above. Cut out.

3. Trace a circle around the face of your pictures. Cut out.

4. Glue the fuchsia flower to the hot pink flower and the teal flower to the purple flower. Glue the pictures to the middles of the fuchsia and teal flowers.

5. Cut the chenille stems so they are not the same height. Glue the chenille stems to the backs of the flowers.

6. Put a dab of glue in the middle of the craft fence and place the ends of the chenille stems into the glue.

23

7. To make a stand, carefully break a craft stick in half. Place broken end of craft stick into dab of glue, between chenille stems. Let all glue dry completely.

You don't need diamonds to have the coolest jewelry! Some basic hardware and craft supplies will make you the envy of all the girls.

Fate chooses our relatives, we choose our friends.
—Jacques Delille

Necklace With Plastic Tubing & Beads

What You'll Need

16 inches clear plastic tubing, ¼ inch diameter

#5 perle cotton floss: purple, orange, and yellow

18-gauge florist wire

4 synthetic bone discs, 10mm each

2 purple pony beads, 14mm each

1 orange pony bead, 16mm

Tool for all projects: heavy-duty or utility scissors

1. Cut tubing into two 8-inch pieces with scissors. Ask an adult for help.

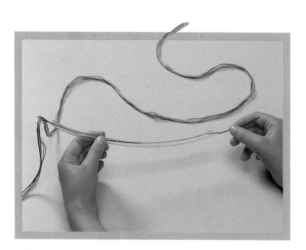

2. Cut two 36-inch strands of each color of floss. Bend a hook in one end of the florist wire and slip all 6 strands of floss through the hook.

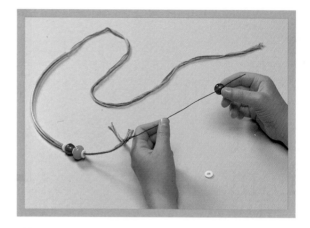

3. Slip wire with floss through a piece of clear tubing. Pull the floss through the tubing. Pull wire and floss through a disc, a purple bead, another disc, the orange bead, a third disc, another purple bead, and the last disc. Slide wire through the second piece of tubing.

4. Adjust and center all the pieces on the floss. Remove floss from wire and tie floss into a knot close to the end of the tubing on each side.

Necklace With Plastic Tubing & Brass Washers

What You'll Need

1 foot clear plastic tubing, ⁵⁄₁₆ inch diameter

Dimensional paint: black and red

1 yard black beading cord

8 brass washers, ¼ inch each

1 foot white opaque plastic tubing, ¼ inch diameter

2 black beads, ¼ inch each

Tools: 7 pencils, glass

1. Using scissors, cut clear tubing into three 1-inch chunks and four ¾-inch chunks.

2. To decorate the plastic chunks with paint, slip a plastic chunk onto the end of a pencil. Squeeze dots of black paint around the 1-inch chunks, holding and rotating the pencil. Stand the pencil in a cup to allow paint to dry. Repeat for remaining 1-inch chunks. Use red paint to squeeze 3 wiggly lines around the ¾-inch chunks, rotating the pencil to make the job easier. Stand pencils in cup to dry.

3. Thread the length of beading cord through the opaque plastic tubing. Over this, slip on a washer, then alternate with a red painted chuck and a black painted chunk onto tubing, slipping a washer between each chunk. End with a washer.

4. Place a black bead on each end of the beading cord and secure it with a knot at both ends of the opaque tubing.

Bracelet With Plastic Tubing & Beads

What You'll Need

12 inches black waxed cord

8 inches clear plastic tubing, ¼ inch diameter

4 synthetic bone discs, 10mm each

2 orange round pony beads, 10mm each

1 purple round pony bead, 14mm

Thread waxed cord through tubing and then the beads in the following order: disc, orange bead, disc, purple bead, disc, orange bead, disc. Tie the ends of the cording tightly together, pulling the tubing into a circle. Double knot the cord and trim tails. Hide the knot inside the beads.

turn the page for more bracelet ideas!

Bracelet With Colored Tubing & Rubber Washers

What You'll Need

*1 foot white opaque plastic tubing,
¼ inch diameter*
Permanent felt markers: pink and green
15 inches waxed cord
9 O flat Bibb washers

Cut tubing into three 4-inch sections. With felt pens, color 4 inches of tubing green and 4 inches of tubing pink. Leave remaining tubing white. Cut 4-inch sections into random lengths from ¼ inch to 1 inch. String tubing on cord alternating colors with the rubber washers. Tie ends of cord together in a double knot. Trim tails.

O Ring Bracelet

What You'll Need

Rubber O rings—sized to fit wrist
Dimensional paint in neon colors
Tin can or glass

Slip O ring over a can or a glass and use paint to decorate the outside edge of the ring with dots and lines. Allow to dry before removing from can.

extra idea!
Fill a toolbox with all the tools and materials you'll need to make jewelry and bring it to your friend's next party. You may even find some odds and ends around the house that you can recycle into some fun and funky jewelry!

What You'll Need

4 colors of embroidery floss, 2½ feet each

Option!

Deli containers with the 6 recycling symbol (or shrink plastic)

Permanent marker pens

Gold metallic elastic thread

Tools: *tape, scissors, pencil, hole punch, aluminum foil, oven*

Hold a true friend with both your hands.
—Nigerian Proverb

charming
friendship
bracelets

Give your friends a special knotted friendship bracelet. Charms add an extra-special look!

29

1. Tie the 4 different colors of embroidery floss together. Tape the knotted end to a table top.

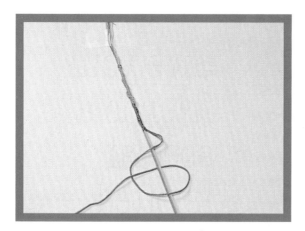

2. Select a color of floss to begin. Make a loop with the floss and bring the end through the loop.

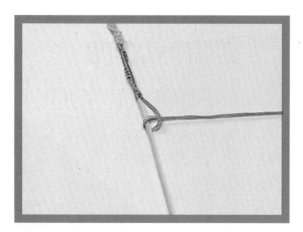

3. Pull the strand tightly to make a knot. Repeat this knot until you have covered about 1 inch, pulling the knots up tightly as you go. The knots will naturally spiral around the inner threads. If you'd like, add charms to your bracelet.

4. To make charms: Place clean, flat pieces of plastic over the patterns on the next page. Trace with a pencil. Using markers, color the backgrounds, then add details and outline. You can also draw designs of your own, making them about the same size as the pattern shapes.

5. Cut the plastic shapes out. Punch a hole in each one, not too close to the edge.

6. Ask an adult to help with this step! Lay plastic shapes on aluminum foil and bake in a 300°F oven for 1 to 2 minutes. The plastic will curl and shrink, then gradually flatten. Remove the charms from the oven when they're almost flat.

7. Cool charms completely, then string them onto your woven bracelet or onto elastic thread, making a knot to tie each charm about ½ inch from the others. Cut the thread after 7 or 8 charms and knot the ends securely.

hip hopping
hair wrapping!

Hair wrapping will create a sensation. Wraps are unique, colorful, and just plain fun. Have a 'rapping good time with a hair wrap party!

I get by with a little help from my friends.
—Paul McCartney

What You'll Need

1 yard of each color of floss you want to use (we used 2 colors)

1. Take a small section of hair (about the width of a penny) from behind the ear along the hairline. Holding both colors together, tie a double knot with the floss around the hair strand. Keep knot as close to the scalp as possible.

2. Split the colors apart. Hold one color and the short ends of floss together with the hair strand. Circle the other long end of floss around behind the strand. Pull the long end of the floss through the loop you just formed. Tighten the knot. This is the wrapping technique.

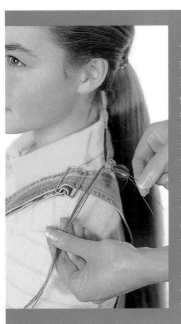

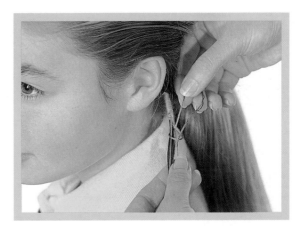

Option!

To add beads, select beads that have a large enough hole to glide onto the hair strand. Use a 6-inch length of bead wire folded in half. Place the bead over the folded end. Thread the hair and the floss through the folded end of the wire and push the bead onto the hair. Pull bottom part of strand through bead and place bead below wrapping.

3. Continue with one color until you are ready to switch colors. Hold the first colored floss along with the hair strand until you're ready to switch again. Pick up the second color and continue to wrap, loop, and tighten. Switch colors as often or as seldom as you want!

33

birds **of a** feather

locker mirror

You look marvelous! To prove it, just look in your locker— at your feathered mirror. Make one for each of your best friends' lockers!

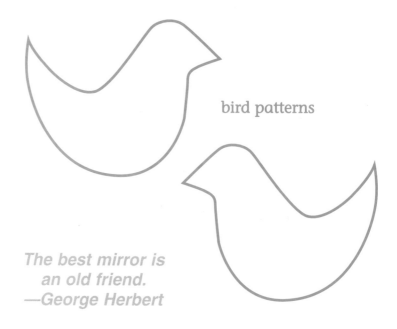

bird patterns

The best mirror is an old friend.
—George Herbert

What You'll Need

Unbreakable mirror
Colorful, small feathers
Scraps of pink and purple fun foam
Magnets
Tools: *craft glue, craft stick, pencil, tracing and white paper, black pen, scissors*

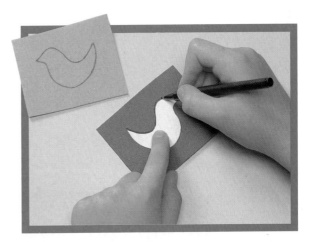

3. Trace the bird pattern on page 34 and then make a white paper pattern. Using a black pen, make a pink and a purple bird.

1. Go through your feathers and arrange how you like them around the mirror. Be sure to vary the colors. Also, starting from the top, use smaller feathers and have them increase in size going to the bottom.

4. Glue the birds to the top of the mirror, slightly overlapping them. Glue a feather to each bird's wing position.

2. Glue the feathers to the mirror.

5. Glue the magnets on the back of the mirror. Depending on how heavy your mirror is, you may want to use more or fewer magnets. We used 5 to hold our mirror up.

pinwheel trinket **jar**

This little jar can hold all your favorite goodies! Use different colors of clay and in different combinations to make a personalized jar for each of your friends.

Friendships multiply joys, and divide griefs.
—Henry George Bohn

extra idea!
Make a pink and red trinket jar for Valentine's Day and fill it with wrapped chocolates. Or as a little birthday surprise for a pal, have all her friends write out happy wishes on brightly colored scraps of paper, and collect them together in a trinket jar! She'll have good wishes to pull out and read all year!

What You'll Need

Polymer clay: green, purple, and pink

Interesting glass jar with metal lid, cleaned with labels removed

Glossy acrylic varnish

***Tools:** waxed paper, tape, rolling pin, craft knife, ruler, oven, flat pan or cookie sheet, paintbrush*

Note: All utensils used for polymer clay should not be used again with food!

3. Pile the sheets of clay on top of each other, with green on the bottom, then purple, then pink. Gently curl a long edge and roll the clays into a jellyroll log with the green clay on the outside.

4. Roll this log back and forth on the table until it stretches out to about 8 inches long.

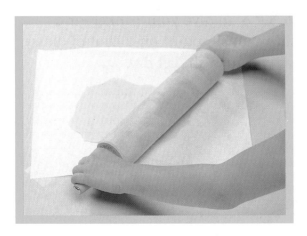

1. Soften clay by squeezing it with your hand. Tape waxed paper onto your surface. Roll each lump of clay into a very thin, flat sheet with the rolling pin.

2. Trim the sheets of clay into rectangles about 3 inches wide and 6 inches long. Make 1 rectangle for each color. Save the clay scraps.

5. With the craft knife, cut the edges of the log so they are even. Then carefully slice thin layers off the log. The slices should be ⅛ inch thick or less.

37

9. Ask an adult for help here! Heat the oven to 325°F. Place your clay-covered jar and lid on a pan and put them into the hot oven. Immediately turn the oven off. Wait 30 minutes, then remove the jar and lid. Let them cool. The clay should now be completely solid. If any clay is still soft, repeat this step.

6. Press these slices all over the outside of the jar, squashing them against the glass with your thumb so they stick firmly. Cover all sides of the jar, but not the bottom. Trim some slices in half to fit along the edges.

10. To give your trinket jar a shiny finish, paint on a coat of glossy acrylic varnish. Let dry.

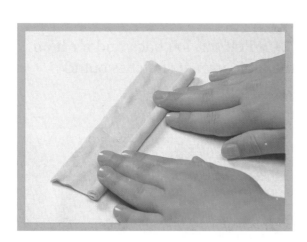

7. Roll your leftover pink clay into a log and make plain pink slices to cover the metal jar lid.

8. Gently screw the lid onto the jar and trim the clay until the lid screws on and off easily.

radical ribbon
address book

What better gift to give a friend who moves away? Write all your friends' names in the book after decorating it with ribbons.

Whoever is happy will make others happy too.
—Anne Frank

What You'll Need

Small address book

Scrap fabric large enough to cover book

6 colors satin ribbon, ½ yard lengths, various widths

Construction paper

Tools: *ruler, pencil, scissors, craft glue, craft stick*

2. Lay the fabric flat on your worktable. Cut pieces of ribbon about 1 inch longer than the long side of the fabric piece. Glue these ribbons right next to each other on the fabric. Use a tiny dot of glue exactly on the center line to hold each ribbon in place. Let glue dry completely.

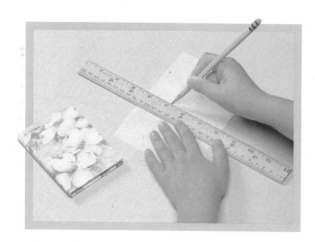

1. Trim the fabric so it wraps around the cover of the address book and fits exactly. Draw a straight line down the middle of the fabric where the book's spine will be.

3. Cut the ribbons to fit across the fabric in the other direction. This time make the ribbon about 1 inch longer than the short side.

extra idea!
Get yourself a pen pal! There's nothing better than getting mail, especially if it's from another town or state or country! This address book would be the perfect gift for a new pen pal who'll admire your creativity!

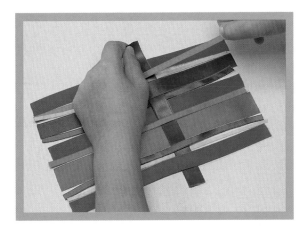

4. Starting in the middle, weave the short ribbon over and under the long ones, pushing the ribbon to the glued center.

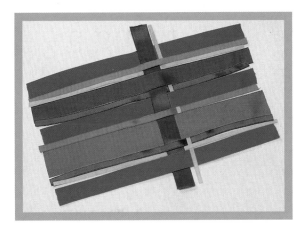

5. Add a second short ribbon next to the first, this time weaving it over the ribbons you went under before, and under the ribbons you went over before. Keep adding ribbon pieces until you've woven all the way to the end of the bottom fabric.

6. Rotate your fabric and weave the other side of the book cover the same way.

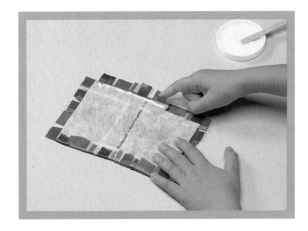

7. Turn fabric over. Glue short ribbon ends down on back.

8. Spread glue down the middle of the fabric. Place the book's spine in the glue. Be sure your fabric covers the book.

9. Fold the long ribbon ends around the book cover and glue them down. Cut 2 pieces of construction paper to fit on the inside faces of the book. Glue the papers down.

happenin'
heart
t-shirt

This would make a great slumber party project. Have each friend bring a T-shirt and you supply the paint!

heart pattern

A friend is someone who knows all about you and loves you anyway.
—Anonymous

What You'll Need

T-shirt

Fabric paint: rose, light blue, light purple, and peach

Dimensional fabric paint: yellow, green, dark purple, rose, light purple, and pink

Tools: *iron, cardboard, sponge, pencil, scissors, disposable plate, paper towels*

1. Prewash T-shirt, but do not use fabric softener. Press out any wrinkles with a warm iron. Place a shirtboard or large piece of cardboard inside the shirt.

3. Using the dimensional paint, outline each heart. We used yellow to outline the rose hearts, green to outline the light blue hearts, dark purple to outline the light purple hearts, and rose to outline the peach hearts. Let paint dry.

2. Using pattern on page 42 as a guide, cut heart out of the sponge. Squirt fabric paint onto plate. Dip heart in paint. If there is too much paint on your sponge, you may want to blot it on paper towels. Position heart on T-shirt carefully and press in place. Using the 4 colors, alternate colors of hearts on T-shirt. Refer to photo if needed. Let paint dry.

4. Make designs inside each heart. You can refer to the photograph if you'd like to copy our shirt. But go ahead and design an original!

5. Let paint dry overnight. For washing instructions and heat setting, follow manufacturer's directions for paint.

Gathering beautiful buttons is a Victorian tradition: Girlfriends traded buttons with each other. Continue the tradition by making pins for all your pals!

button bouquet brooches

What You'll Need

2 green chenille stems, 12 inches each

5 beautiful buttons

12 inches ribbon, ¾ inch wide

¾-inch pin back

Tools: *scissors, ruler, needlenose pliers, glue gun, glue sticks*

1. Cut the chenille stems into 4-inch lengths.

2. For flat buttons, slip a stem through a button hole, going from the back and then through the front to the back again. Twist the stem tightly at the back using the needlenose pliers. For post-style buttons, twist the stem through the hole, then add a drop of hot glue to hold the button so it faces forward.

True friendship is a plant of slow growth.
—George Washington

3. Gather the 5 chenille stems together and wrap them tightly with the last 4-inch chenille stem. Trim the ends of the wrapped stem.

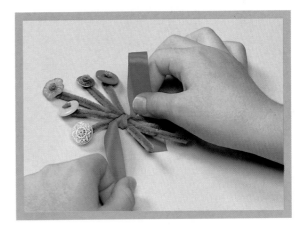

4. Bend the button flowers gracefully to make a flat bouquet. Pull some of the flower stems shorter, leaving others longer. Trim the bottom of the stems. Tie the ribbon in a bow around the center of your bouquet.

5. Glue a pin back to the back of the bouquet.

button
buddies

To like and dislike the same things, that is indeed true friendship.
—Sallust

These fun and fanciful guys will jazz up any blouse! Make one that looks like you and one like your best friend. Or make a cat and a dog. The possibilities are endless!

What You'll Need

Sueded leatherette fabric (or smooth leatherette)

Permanent markers

Tools: *pencil, tracing paper, transfer paper, scissors, craft knife*

2. Color in design with permanent markers. (Test the markers on a small piece of the fabric to be sure they don't smear.) You can copy our coloring, or you can make the girls resemble you and your best friend.

1. Trace patterns on page 48. Cut a small piece of fabric a bit larger than each pattern. Lay transfer paper between the pattern and the fabric (transfer side down). Trace pattern onto fabric.

3. Outline all shapes with the black marker.

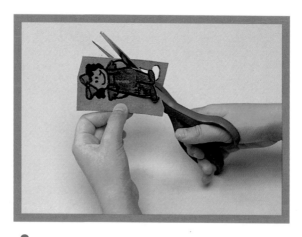

4. Cut the shape out. Cut the slit for the button with the craft knife. Ask an adult to help you when you work with a craft knife!